TOUCANS

by Mary Ann McDonald

The Child's World

Content Adviser:
David A. Oehler,
Curator of Birds,
Cincinnati Zoo &
Botanical Garden

Published in the United States of America by The Child's World®
PO Box 326 • Chanhassen, MN 55317-0326
800-599-READ • www.childsworld.com

PHOTO CREDITS
© Art Wolfe/Getty Images: 16, 21, 27
© Danita Delimont/Alamy: 15
© Joseph Van Os/Getty Images: 8
© Kevin Schafer: cover, 1
© Mark J. Thomas/Dembinsky Photo Associates: 7
© Medioimages/Alamy: 22
© Pete Oxford/Minden Pictures: 24–25
© Stephen Dalton/Minden Pictures: 29
© Steve Bloom Images/Alamy: 11
© Theo Allofs/Corbis: 5, 9
© Tom Brakefield/Corbis: 19
© VEER John Giustina/Getty Images: 12–13

ACKNOWLEDGMENTS
The Child's World®: Mary Berendes, Publishing Director;
Katherine Stevenson, Editor

The Design Lab: Kathleen Petelinsek, Design and Page Production

LIBRARY OF CONGRESS CATALOGING-IN-PUBLICATION DATA
McDonald, Mary Ann.
 Toucans / by Mary Ann McDonald.
   p. cm. — (New naturebooks)
 Includes bibliographical references and index.
 ISBN 1-59296-652-7 (library bound : alk. paper)
 1. Toucans—Juvenile literature. I. Title. II. Series.
 QL696.P57M35 2006
 598.7'2—dc22   2006001379

Table of Contents

On the cover: When people think of toucans, they often picture toco toucans like this one. Toco toucans are known for their bright orange bills.

Meet the Toucan!

Toucans are related to woodpeckers and another group of birds called *barbets*.

Deep in a rain forest, animals of all kinds are moving around. On the ground, ants march in a line as they gather food for their nest. A bright green snake slithers along a fallen log. Insects hum and buzz through the air. High in a tree, a strange bird hops along. It stands firmly on a branch, then reaches way out to pick some fruit with its huge, colorful beak. What could this strange bird be? It's a toucan!

This toco toucan is peeking down from its perch in Brazil's Pantanal Matogrossense National Park. The park is a protected area that covers over 541 square miles (1,400 sq km).

What Are Toucans?

Male toucans often have larger bills than females.

The keel-billed toucan is the national bird of the country of Belize.

Toucans are a group of birds that have bright markings and an enormous beak or bill. The bill is fairly flat on both sides. Its edges are **serrated**— sharp and jagged like a saw blade or a bread knife. Toucans' bills come in yellow, white, green, red, brown, blue, black, or often a combination of colors.

Toucans' bodies are fairly heavy, and their wings are short and somewhat rounded. Like many other birds, toucans like to sit, or perch, on branches. Their short, sturdy legs support their heavy bodies when they perch, and their wide tails help them balance.

Keel-billed toucans are known for their beautiful bills, which are often lime green with other bright colors. These toucans are about 20 inches (51 cm) long and are found in forests from Mexico to Colombia.

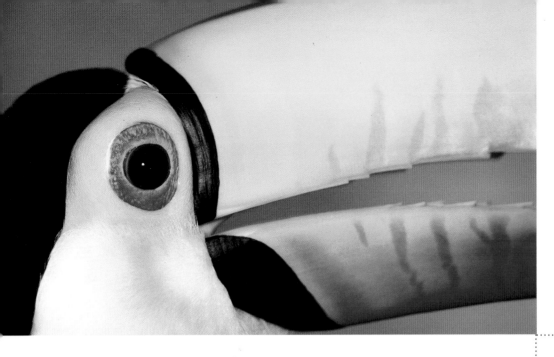

The eyes of toco toucans are surrounded by brilliant blue skin.

There are about 40 different kinds, or **species**, of toucans. The smallest are only about seven inches (18 cm) long. The biggest are toco toucans, which are about 25 inches (64 cm) long and weigh about a pound (.5 kg).

Like all birds, toucans have feathers, or **plumage**, all over their bodies. Some of the best-known toucan species have black plumage with yellow or white on their throats and chests. Near their eyes, toucans have bare skin that is often brightly colored, making the birds even more beautiful.

Scientists are still trying to decide exactly how many species of toucans there are and how they are related to other, similar birds.

Toucans are divided into three groups— toucans, *toucanets*, and *araçaris* (ar-uh-SAR-ees).

Channel-billed toucans like this one are part of a group called black toucans. *These toucans have bills that are mostly black. Channel-billed toucans live mainly in South America.*

Where Do Toucans Live?

When many toucans fly, they look as if they are riding a roller coaster—flap, flap, glide . . . flap, flap, glide. When they flap their wings, they rise a little higher. When they glide, they sink slowly toward the ground.

Some toucans in mountainous areas live as high up as 9,000 feet (2,743 m) above sea level.

Toucans live in Central and South America, from Mexico all the way down to Argentina. Most of them live in forests, and many live in **tropical** rain forests. They usually live high up in the trees. Smaller toucans fly through the trees quickly and easily. Larger, heavier toucans don't fly as easily. Instead, they move through the trees mostly by hopping along tree branches and jumping from one branch to another.

Most birds have three toes that point forward and one that points backward. But toucans, like woodpeckers, have two toes that face backward and two that face forward. The toucans' feet and strong toes are perfect for climbing through tree branches.

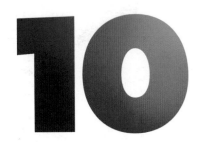

Here you can see a toco toucan as it flies toward the photographer. Toco toucans live mainly in the warm forests of South America.

What Do Toucans Eat?

Toucans almost never land on the ground. They drink from puddles of rainwater in the forks of trees or huge leaves.

Toucans swallow fruits and berries whole, then spit up the seeds. They help spread the seeds of many plants.

Toucans eat lots of different things. They are **omnivores**, which means they eat both plants and animals. Fruit is their favorite. Luckily, there is plenty of fruit where they live! Toucans also eat insects, frogs, spiders, lizards, and snakes. If they get the chance, they even steal eggs and babies from other birds' nests. These animal foods provide protein that helps keep the toucans strong.

Toucans use their bills to squash the fruits they eat. They also use the serrated edges to rip bites off bigger fruits. Inside the bill, the toucan's tongue is long and narrow, with feathery edges that help the bird taste its foods.

This toco toucan has found a large nut to eat. This picture also shows the serrated sides of the toucan's bill.

Why Do Toucans Have Such Large Bills?

A toco toucan's bill is up to eight inches (20 cm) long—about one-third of the toucan's total length.

Moving food along such a long bill isn't easy! Toucans often toss their food up in the air, then catch it and gulp it down.

Scientists aren't quite sure why toucans have such big bills, but they have several ideas. One idea has to do with reaching foods. Because toucans are fairly heavy, they must sit on strong, thick branches. But strong branches often don't have fruit growing on them. The toucan's long bill lets the bird pluck fruits and berries from other branches while sitting in a safe spot.

The size and bright colors of toucans' bills might also help the birds attract mates. They probably help keep the birds safe, too, by making the toucans look bigger than they really are. **Predators** looking for animals to eat might think twice before they bother such a big, colorful bird!

This toco toucan is using its long bill to reach a papaya fruit in Brazil.

Toucan's bills are interesting on the inside. They look very heavy, but they are actually very light. In fact, they are mostly air! Even so, they don't break easily. Scientists have been studying them to see how they can be so light, yet so strong. Inside, the bills are like a sponge, with large air pockets separated by very thin walls. The bills are supported by thin, criss-crossed rods of bony material. On the outside, toucans' bills are covered with plates of *keratin*. Keratin is the same substance that makes up cows' horns and your fingernails and hair.

Scientists think they might be able to use what they're learning about toucans' bills to make lighter, stronger, and safer airplanes and cars.

This keel-billed toucan's bill looks very different from the front!

Do Toucans Live Alone?

When toucan flocks fly, they often play follow-the-leader. One toucan takes the lead, and the others straggle along in a line behind it.

Toucans are **social animals**—they like the company of other toucans. In fact, almost all toucans spend their lives with at least one other bird. Many kinds of toucans live in small groups. They do everything together, from eating to sleeping to playing.

Toucans are smart. They're also the clowns of the tropical forests. They play "king of the branch" with each other. The winner is whichever bird forces the other one to move backwards on the branch. They have pretend swordfights with their beaks. Sometimes they even play catch! One bird tosses a piece of fruit into the air, and another one snatches it up.

18

Here you can see two toco toucans as they rest in a dead tree on a sunny day.

Where Do Toucans Nest?

Both toucans and woodpeckers are called *cavity nesters* because they make their nests in holes or hollows.

Many wild toucans are very protective of their nests. It's hard for scientists to take photos or study toucans while they are nesting.

Toucans nest high above the ground, in a hole or **cavity** in a tree. The best nesting cavities are surrounded by solid wood and have a small entrance, just big enough for the adults to squeeze through. The small entrance makes it harder for other animals to get in. Sometimes toucans find a natural cavity, and sometimes they use a hole made by woodpeckers. Sometimes they kick the woodpeckers out of a cavity and take it over! Once they find a good nest, some toucans will use it for years.

Unlike many other birds, toucans don't line their nests with anything soft or fluffy. Sometimes the nest has a few loose, leftover wood chips in the bottom. And sometimes the bottom of the nest gets covered with seeds the toucans have eaten and thrown up.

This toco toucan is watching for danger from its nest in Brazil.

Toucans sleep in an unusual way, and no one is sure why. Some people think it's because at least some toucan species sleep in cramped nesting cavities. Many different kinds of birds turn their heads backwards when they sleep. They tuck their beaks down into their feathers and get comfortable. Toucans do that as well, laying their big beaks along their backs. But they also fold their tails up over their backs and beaks. They look kind of like lawn chairs folded up for storage!

With several adult toucans sleeping in the same small nest, folding their tails up and out of the way would make good sense!

The chestnut-mandibled toucan in this picture is grooming its feathers. When it's ready to take a nap, it turns its head a little farther than it's doing here. Then it lays its bill on its back, folds its tail over the top, and goes to sleep!

How Are Baby Toucans Born?

Parent toucans take turns warming and protecting the eggs, but they don't keep them covered all the time, as some birds do. Sometimes, both parents are gone from the nest.

Predators steal baby toucans from the nest if they can. Sometimes none of the toucan babies survive.

After mating with a male, the female toucan lays one to four white, glossy eggs. The parents take turns keeping the eggs warm. When the babies hatch, usually between two and three weeks later, they are blind and have no feathers. Their bills are fairly small. They depend on their parents to protect them and care for them. The parents spit up recently eaten food for the babies to eat.

Each day, the baby toucans get a little bigger and stronger. They begin to grow plumage just like the adults'. About six to eight weeks after they hatch, the babies are ready to fly from the nest. It might be several more months before their bills are fully grown and fully colored.

Here you can see a plate-billed mountain toucan as it brings its baby some food. These rare toucans live in the higher areas of Colombia and Ecuador.

Can Toucans Sing?

When toucans call, their bills swoop quickly upward.

A toucan's call is loud! A croaking sound from a toucan can be heard a half-mile (almost 1 km) away.

Toucans are noisy, but they don't sing like lots of other birds. Instead, they make other kinds of sounds. Depending on what kind of toucans they are, they croak like frogs, chirp, and yelp. Some make loud rattles and short, high barking sounds, too. Toucan cries echo throughout the forest all day long.

If toucans sense danger, they get excited and make faster, louder noises. If a group of toucans sees an enemy nearby, the birds all scream and squawk. That's usually enough to make the enemy go away.

Here you can see a toco toucan as it calls in a Brazilian forest.

Are Toucans in Danger?

In Central and South America, some people think of toucans as bad spirits or bringers of bad luck.

Keel-billed toucans have been known to live for 15 to 20 years.

Throughout Central and South America, tropical forests are being destroyed for farming and building. Loss of these areas, or **environments**, has harmed many kinds of plants and animals, including toucans. Destroying the forests leaves less food and fewer places for animals to live. Some toucan species are also rare because they are hunted for food or their colorful feathers. Some birds are also captured and sent to other countries so people can keep them as pets.

Toucans aren't yet in danger of dying out, but their future is uncertain. If we all work to preserve the forests where they live, these colorful birds will be with us for a long time to come.

Red-billed toucans like this one are also called white-throated toucans. They live in Colombia, Bolivia, and Brazil.

28

Glossary

cavity (KA-vih-tee) A cavity is a hole or hollowed-out area. Toucans nest in cavities in trees.

environments (en-VY-run-munts) Environments are the kinds of places in which plants or animals live, including the land, other plants and animals, water, and weather. Many environments where toucans live are being destroyed.

omnivores (OM-nih-vorz) Omnivores are animals that eat both plants and animals. Toucans are omnivores.

plumage (PLOO-mij) Plumage is a bird's covering of feathers. Toucans are known for their beautiful plumage.

predators (PREH-duh-terz) Predators are animals that hunt and kill other animals for food. Predators sometimes eat baby toucans.

serrated (seh-RAY-ted) Something that is serrated has a notched or jagged edge, like a saw blade. A toucan's bill has serrated edges.

social animals (SOH-shull A-nuh-mullz) Social animals are animals that like to be with others of their own kind. Toucans are social animals.

species (SPEE-sheez) An animal species is a group of animals that share the same features and can have babies only with animals in the same group. There are about 40 different species of toucans.

tropical (TRAH-pih-kull) Tropical areas are those that have warm, moist weather all year long. Toucans live in tropical areas of Central and South America.

To Find Out More

Read It!

Dollar, Sam. *Toucans.* Austin, TX: Steadwell Books, 2001.

McKee, David. *Two Can Toucan.* London, Andersen, 2001.

Miller, Sara Swan. *Woodpeckers, Toucans, and Their Kin.* Danbury, CT: Franklin Watts, 2003.

On the Web

Visit our home page for lots of links about toucans:
http://www.childsworld.com/links

Note to Parents, Teachers, and Librarians: We routinely check our Web links to make sure they're safe, active sites—so encourage your readers to check them out!

Index

About the Author

Mary Ann McDonald is a professional wildlife photographer who lives in central Pennsylvania with her husband Joe, also a photographer and writer. For the past 17 years, she has photographed wildlife around the world, from Rwanda to Chile to Yellowstone National Park. Mary Ann and Joe teach photography workshops at their home, which they call Hoot Hollow. Mary Ann's photographs have appeared in many national and international publications, including Ranger Rick, Your Big Back Yard *and* National Geographic Kids.